Pagan Portals
Hoodoo
Folk Magic

Pagan Portals
Hoodoo
Folk Magic

Rachel Patterson

Winchester, UK
Washington, USA

First published by Moon Books, 2013
Moon Books is an imprint of John Hunt Publishing Ltd., Laurel House, Station Approach,
Alresford, Hants, SO24 9JH, UK
office1@jhpbooks.net
www.johnhuntpublishing.com
www.moon-books.net

For distributor details and how to order please visit the 'Ordering' section on our website.

A CIP catalogue record for this book is available from the British Library.

Design: Stuart Davies

Printed and bound by CPI Group (UK) Ltd, Croydon, CR0 4YY

We operate a distinctive and ethical publishing philosophy in all
areas of our business, from our global network of authors to
production and worldwide distribution.

CONTENTS

Foreword: Who am I?

My craft name is Tansy Firedragon. I have been a witch for many years now and have studied many areas within the Craft.

I am High Priestess in my own coven co-run by my lovely sisters in the Craft, the Kitchen Witch Coven of Natural Witchery, as well as being a member of the Dorset Grove Druids, which allows me to attend lots of outside rituals in wonderful sacred places within the UK.

I am co-founder and a leadership team member of the online Kitchen Witch School of Natural Witchcraft.

My personal website: www.rachelpatterson.co.uk
My email: tansyfiredragon@yahoo.com
My blog: www.tansyfiredragon.blogspot.co.uk
My facebook page: www.facebook.com/racheltansypatterson
My twitter page: www.twitter.com/tansyfiredragon
The Kitchen Witch School website:
www.kitchenwitchhearth.com
The Kitchen Witch School facebook page:
www.facebook.com/kitchenwitchuk
The Kitchen Witch blog: www.kitchenwitchuk.blogspot.co.uk

Introduction

Now, I am not a born and bred hereditary Hoodoo root worker living in Georgia or New Orleans (I hope to come back in another lifetime as one though...), but I have studied Hoodoo in great detail. I work with Hoodoo magic all the time and have incorporated it into my witchcraft. I have great respect for the practice of Hoodoo and all the practitioners who use it.

What I hope to do in this book is provide an introduction to this amazing and fascinating magical practice.

This is MY interpretation of Hoodoo and how I work with it within the Craft. I have tried to make it as accurate as possible and have drawn on many sources as well as my own experiences. I have included many original recipes for oils, powders, incenses etc and have tried to be as traditional as possible with the ingredients for the well known ones, but other recipes included here are my own blends and therefore may not be so traditional.

My intention is for this book to honour the art of Hoodoo and all those who practise it.

Chapter I

What is Hoodoo?

Hoodoo in the form that we know it can be traced back to the early 19th Century, and possibly earlier. Hoodoo is the American name for African American folk magic.

Many religions sprang from the African traditions, such as Yoruba, Santeria, Vodoun and Candomblé. Hoodoo came out of those beliefs and is the magical practice, not an actual religion. It is definitely not Voodoo, as it is commonly called by mistake. Voodoo, or Vodou, is a Haitian African religion, while Vodoun is West African.

Hoodoo as we recognise it was established during the times of slavery in America using the native plants and items available to the people at the time and probably taking a little knowledge from the Native Americans too, with definitely some European folk magic thrown in to the mix as well. I do believe a good amount of the Hoodoo magical practices were brought by slaves; they didn't arrive as slaves with no beliefs or practices at all!

A lot of the slaves at the time were forced to follow the Catholic religion. What they did was to incorporate the saints, deities and rituals into their own religion. Santeria is a good example of this, although they also included the darker side of magic such as curses and hexes as well.

If you take a look into the blues music from the times of slavery you will find a huge amount of references to Hoodoo in the lyrics.

Hoodoo is a practice of magic which is based on surviving and the need for things such as healing using herbs, plants, roots, stones, minerals and the like, combined with chants, rituals and handmade items. It is based around a main framework of intents – love, success, luck, happiness, health and wealth. It is also a form of magic that works with one's own personal power.

However, I suspect that those practitioners of Hoodoo in America rarely call it by a name, it is just what they do, what they grew up doing, what their mothers and grandmothers did. Hoodoo is often referred to by other names such as 'conjure' or 'root work' in fact a practitioner of this magical practice is often called a root worker or conjurer and sometimes referred to as a Hoodoo Doctor.

Like a lot of magical practices, Hoodoo uses the magical properties of natural items including traditional herbs, roots and minerals, but it also makes use of animal parts and bodily fluids. (No, don't worry you won't have to bash any wild animals, but you will be able to use bones from your Sunday lunch roast chicken or, if you aren't too squeamish, road kill!)

The practice includes such things as jinxing, foot track magic, crossroads magic and laying tricks. Foot track magic works with the essence of the person by using their footprints. Crossroads magic works by leaving magical items at a crossroads (no surprise there!) or a place where two roads intersect. Crossroads are magical places and always have been. Probably the most well known item for a Hoodoo practitioner to use is a mojo bag, but in Hoodoo the use of candles, incense, oils, powders, talismans and spiritual washes is also common.

Originally those who worked with Hoodoo would probably have used whatever they could get their hands on, using lamps and plain white candles for spell work, dressing them only with blessed olive oil and using basic items and ingredients that they had to hand.

At some point in the history of Hoodoo, which my research seems to suggest having been about the time of the American Civil War, people started to 'market' oils, coloured candles and vinegars; giving them the fantastic names that we now associate with Hoodoo products. But as with most magical practices my advice would be, use what seems right to you and use what you have to hand and what your intuition and instinct tell you is right. You don't need to splash out huge amounts of cash on branded products; you can make most things you need yourself. If you do purchase items from a shop or online I would just suggest you check out their credentials first and what ingredients they use; there are some wonderful retailers out there, but there are some bad ones too.

Come take a walk with me through the magical art of Hoodoo...

Chapter 2

Root Work

Root work is another name for Hoodoo; its practitioners are often referred to as root workers. It refers to the understanding of herbs and nature and, in particular, the belief that the root of a plant holds its power and spirit; plant roots being an important part of Hoodoo magical practice.

What is Used?

The practice of Hoodoo uses many things, some natural items that the Earth provides and some that are not so natural! Basically, a Hoodoo practitioner will use what they have to hand. If they have natural items such as twigs and bones they will use them, but if they need to they will also use items such as bleach and ammonia.

Ashe

Ashe is the magical element, the spirit, the power that is inside all natural things – stones, herbs, bones etc. Even when we speak a chant the words contains ashe. It is a power.

Graveyard Dirt

Don't be afraid of going into a graveyard, they are usually beautiful, peaceful and spiritual places.

Graveyard dirt is used a lot in Hoodoo. It is a connection to the dead and a link to our ancestors. To obtain it there is an accepted process of events. First you must connect with the spirit of the person whose grave you would like to take the dirt from and then you must very respectfully ask their permission. You will also need to leave some sort of offering in payment for the dirt you take. You also need to check whose grave you are taking dirt from as well. Dirt from the grave of a soldier who died in battle will work differently from that of someone who died at the age of 90 peacefully in their sleep.

Offerings you might like to leave on the grave would be small coins, flowers or maybe alcohol depending again on the person who lies therein. Leaving a tot of whiskey for a teetotal school ma'am probably wouldn't go down so well...

Get to know your local graveyard, get the feel of it, make several visits there and see who you can connect with first before you even attempt to take graveyard dirt. Have a wander around the place and see what graves reach out to you (hopefully not literally). You may find that you are subconsciously pulled towards certain graves. Connect with the ancestors there. Always be respectful and always ask first. The spirits will most likely tell you what they want.

Graveyard dirt is particularly useful in protection and love spells, but is also used in binding spells as well. The dirt can be used for harmful tricks, the graveyard dirt signifying in this case – death.

Graveyard dirt has power because it is so directly linked with the spirits of the dead, those of our ancestors.

What I would say as a caution, especially for those new to Hoodoo, is to avoid collecting dirt from graves that contain murder victims and those who died unjustly. These spirits may harbour unhealthy vengeful energies.

On the same theme as graveyard dirt there is also the use of coffin nails. Originally coffins would be dug up in order to retrieve the nails from them, but I would advise against this, not only because it is illegal and I would hate for you to be sent to jail and because coffins don't tend to have proper nails in any more, but also because I feel it is incredibly disrespectful to the person lying within the coffin! A good substitute is to use rusty nails.

Rusty nails can be used in spells against your enemies, but also for protection.

Fluids

If you are a bit squeamish this section probably isn't for you and it is possible to work incredibly powerful Hoodoo magic without these items, but it is a part of the magical practice so I have included it here for reference and just in case you want to give it a try...

Bodily fluids, hair, nail clippings and the like have been used in magical practices, not just Hoodoo, for centuries. It is a very definite way of connecting your spell or trick to a particular person. Witch bottles found in the UK lodged into walls or buried under the doorsteps of old buildings were found to contain human hair, nail clippings and urine.

Think about fluids such as menstrual blood and semen – both of these link directly to sex and fertility so logic says that they would make excellent ingredients in love or fertility tricks.

You may never drink another cup of coffee after this information but... menstrual blood is used to gain sexual attraction from a man, just pop a drop or two into his morning cuppa and the trick is worked. If you have a willing and adventurous partner, in Hoodoo the practice of feeding him your menstrual blood with his knowledge is a way of binding him to you and keeping him faithful.

Equally a man can use his semen in a similar fashion. By placing some of his semen in a drink given to his chosen woman, the man is setting a trick in motion to capture her sexual attraction to him. On the flipside of this, if a woman captures some of a man's semen she can then use it in spell working to bind him, keep him faithful and control him.

And then we have urine; used for centuries in European folk magic and also used in Hoodoo. It makes a good substitute if you don't have menstrual blood or semen as it is a very personal fluid and links directly to its owner. In Hoodoo urine is often referred to as 'chamber lye' or just simply 'water' – be wary next time someone offers you a glass of 'water'! The word 'chamber' originates from the old chamber pot that was kept under the bed for people to relieve themselves in during the night and 'lye' is an old Anglo Saxon word meaning a strong liquid with high alkaline content.

Chamber lye (doesn't that sound nicer than urine?) is often used for luck. A person who needs some fast luck, maybe for some quick money or in a card game, will ask a willing female to add their chamber lye to their mojo bag. This is in essence 'feeding' the mojo bag with luck. It seems to only be a female's chamber lye that is lucky though…

What you don't want though is an enemy to get hold of any of your bodily fluids. They can then use these to lay tricks against you, causing you all sorts of grief and harm.

If all the above leaves you feeling a bit wary, how about using something like leftover bath water? Or even a half-drunk cup of coffee? These liquids will hold a connection to the person who used them.

There are many items that can be used if you don't want to go down the 'bodily fluid' road, such as locks of hair, nail clippings, a used piece of clothing, handwriting on a piece of paper, an item the person has worn or touched, cigarette butts, photographs or even their business card.

Herbs and Roots

All sorts of herbs are used in Hoodoo magic, all of the usual household ones along with a few more unusual ones. I haven't included a complete list here as it would go on forever, but here are some of the more popular ones used in Hoodoo.

Adam and Eve Root (Putty Root/Aplectrum)

This root was used a lot in Adam and Eve magic, believed to promote true love and a good strong equal partnership between a couple. It was also used for sexual problems within a relationship. However, Adam and Eve root is now endangered and should no longer be harvested from the wild. Unfortunately, there isn't a substitute for the root either, so be aware if you purchase 'Adam and Eve' products because they probably won't have the true ingredients.

Alfalfa
This is a herb used for prosperity and money draw spells. It can be sprinkled into your purse, kept in your money box or used as a powder.

Angelica Root (Holy Ghost/Archangel Root)
This has many uses within Hoodoo – warding off evil, boosting luck, health, family matters, peace, strength (especially for women), uncrossing, jinx breaking and as a powerful guardian.

Buckeye Nuts
Useful for gamblers, luck and sexual power. (In the UK you could substitute a conker).

Clover
Clover is probably used all over the world for luck! Within Hoodoo it is also used for prosperity and money draw spells. It is also considered sacred in that having three leaves it represents the trinity.

Coconut
Coconut is used for domination within Hoodoo, a whole coconut often being used to represent the victim's head and mind.

Devil's Dung (Asafoetida)
You've got to love the folk name for this one! It is a very strong smelling powder (hence the name) and is used in Hoodoo for protection, banishing, curses and working against your enemies. (When handling asafoetida I recommend wearing gloves...

otherwise you will carry the scent on your hands for ages!)

Devil's Shoestring (Viburnum Alnifolium, Opulus, Prunifolium)

These 'shoestrings' are roots from the plant and are used for protection, luck, job seeking and keeping out the devil – the 'shoestring' is meant to trip him up!

Five-Finger Grass (Cinquefoil/Potentilla)

The plant has five leaves that are segmented and look a bit like a hand – hence the name five-finger grass. It is used for luck, gambling, money drawing, employment and favours.

High John the Conqueror Root (Ipomoea Jalapa, Purge, Pandurata)

High John the Conqueror root is one of the main herbs used in Hoodoo magic.

The story goes that John was a prince, son of an African king, and that he dedicated himself to helping others, those who were tricked by their white masters. He is a trickster spirit and also a hero of folklore.

The roots that carry his name are: High John, Dixie John and Little John. High John is said to carry the trickster's spirit within it.

High John the Conqueror root brings with it the magical properties of power, prosperity, strength, luck, love and the ability to conquer all within its path.

Lettuce

Lettuce is used mainly in money draw spells. You can use any type of lettuce, but make sure the leaves are fresh; the best ones are the darker outside leaves. Greens can be used in the same way.

Mint

This is used mainly for money drawing, prosperity, uncrossing or to cool and calm a situation or person.

Orris Root (Queen Elizabeth Root)

Used in Hoodoo by women and men to attract and control a man.

Pepper

All sorts of pepper varieties are used in Hoodoo magic. Black pepper is good for protection, banishing, curses and enemy spells; red pepper (cayenne) is good for protection, banishing, curses, enemy spells and also to add heat (and therefore power) to spells too.

Rue

Used mainly in protection spells, but also for love. Wearing a sprig of rue will ward off the 'evil eye'.

Spanish Moss

Used in spells working against your enemy and revenge spells. Also often used to stuff doll babies (poppets).

Violet

Used in powders, incense and foot track magic for innocence, purity, chastity, feminine issues and concerns of a sexual nature.

Willow

This is a good all-round herb. The leaves of the willow are used for love, luck, health and protection.

Witch Grass (Dog Grass/Devil's Grass/Couch Grass/Twitch Grass)

Used for love, break-up and enemy spells and also good for

stuffing doll babies (poppets).

Animal Parts

Animal parts are used quite often in Hoodoo magic, but I think it is an area that is quite often misunderstood or misinterpreted or just plain hyped up by the media because it makes a good story.

Some practitioners would never harm an animal (I am one of them). However, I don't see a problem with working with animal parts that have either died a natural death, were killed for food or were the unfortunate victims of a fatal road accident. Others may never harm an animal even for food, nor use any animal parts – it is a personal choice.

Some practitioners may feel OK with killing such things as insects, spiders and snails for instance, but would never harm anything larger.

Some practitioners will have no issues at all with despatching an animal themselves and using all the parts in their work... I do not advocate this behaviour, never have and never will. To harm an animal for the purpose of magical work is not acceptable in my view.

OK now we have got that out of the way...

Bones in particular carry with them the ashe, the spirit, the power of the animal that they belonged to. I have a magpie skull, wing and feet that were collected from an animal that was killed by a car. A friend dried the wing and feet under a baker's oven for me (so that all the pests and nasties were cleared from it) and I buried the skull in the garden to let the insects clean all of the icky bits from it. (Just remember where you buried it!) When I dug it up a couple of weeks later it was beautifully clean. I use these items in spell work when I need the magical properties that the magpie carries with it.

Chicken bones, for instance, can be used after you have eaten your roast chicken for lunch, the same with any fowl that you cook and eat. Utilise the bones rather than throwing them away, that way you are using as much of the animal as you can, which makes sense (to me anyway). They are excellent for soaking up negative energy.

If you don't like the idea of working with real bones, but want to use the energy of a particular animal, the black cat for instance which is used a lot within Hoodoo, you can use a hair or two from the animal instead.

Please I urge you… only use the bones of an animal if you know where it came from and how it died. There are a lot of scam artists out there on the internet, some selling fake items and some selling items that have come from sources you probably don't want to know about.

The shed skin of a snake can be powdered and used in powders, especially goofer dust. The rattlesnake is the preferred snake species, but others can be used. Rattlesnake dust is also used in spells to reverse bad luck or jinxes.

A rabbit's foot is considered lucky in a lot of traditions across the world and although not so easy to get hold of now they are still a part of Hoodoo magic.

Brooms

A Hoodoo practitioner will always have a broom! They are used to sweep the floors as well as sweeping people. To cleanse the house or dispel negative energy the broom is used to sweep from the back of the house to the front. To cleanse a person they are swept from their head down to their feet. To bring positive energy, the house is swept from the front to the back and the same goes for a person. They are swept from their feet up to their head usually with a smaller hand-held broom often made from chicken feathers.

The sweeping action is specific; the broom is used in one direction only. Do one sweep then pick up the broom and sweep again in the same direction. And while the sweeping is being done focus must be made; concentration is set on the intent as the broom makes its moves.

Cowry Shells

A favourite in Hoodoo magic, the cowry shell represents the female genitalia (you only have to look at the shape of the shell to see it). It therefore symbolises the feminine divine, female energy and the idea of rebirth along with cleansing and new beginnings. Originally these shells would have been used as currency.

Minerals/Metals/Lodestones

Many minerals and metals are used in Hoodoo.

Lodestones are used because of their magnetic powers. They are used to attract and draw whatever the practitioner desires to them.

To Make Lodestone Oil

Put a lodestone and a pinch of magnetic sand in a small bottle and fill it up with a base oil (olive, almond the choice is yours). You can add a drop or two of an essential oil if you wish. Seal the bottle, give it a shake and leave it for three to four weeks.

Magnetic oil can be achieved by following the above instructions but using a small magnet instead of the lodestone. (For more on oils, see the Oils chapter.)

Lodestone Sachet Powder

Put a lodestone and a pinch of magnetic sand into a small bottle or jar, and then fill it up with talcum powder or corn flour (corn starch). Seal the bottle and leave for three to four weeks.

Magnetic sachet powder can be made by following the above instructions, but using a magnet instead of the lodestone. (For more on powders, see the Powders chapter.)

Alum

Alum is used in Hoodoo for luck and protection. In its powdered form it can be used to stop gossip and back stabbing. Write the victim's name on a slip of paper and put it into a small jar containing alum, state your intent and bury the jar.

Brass
Brass is a very good metal to use in love drawing spells.

Brimstone
Brimstone, or sulphur, is used in rock and powder form and always makes me think of demonic forces! In Hoodoo it is used to protect from evil, to banish evil and in spells against your enemies. (Warning: don't burn sulphur as it can produce very toxic gas.)

Copper
Copper is a good metal to use as a conduit for energy and also good for luck, money draw spells and healing.

Iron
Iron is excellent for protection spells and represents the warrior spirit.

Magnetic Sand (Anvil Dust)
Used to sprinkle on lodestones to 'feed' their energy. It is also used in love drawing, luck and money drawing spells. Magnetic sand is actually fine black sand like grains of iron.

Silver
Good for intuition, dreams, fertility, love and any kind of sea or moon magic. Silver is also good for breaking hexes.

Salt
Salt is such a useful natural substance and is incredibly protective by nature. Basic table salt can be used or any of the sea

or rock salts. Used on its own it is protective and purifying, but it is also a good base ingredient for powders and washes. In Hoodoo it is a key ingredient not only for protection but also in breaking evil and enemy spells and undoing tricks.

Black salt is used in Hoodoo a lot and is used to remove or dispel negativity and evil and to banish people. It can also be used in curses.

Black salt is made up from normal white salt, but then powdered charcoal is added, or ash in some cases. If you can't get hold of ash or charcoal you can mix black pepper with the salt for a similar end result.

Sprinkle black salt on your floors then sweep it out from the back of the house to the front to dispel negativity from your home.

If you have a guest you really don't ever want to return to your house again, once they leave sprinkle black salt on your porch and then sweep it quickly out away from your house, cursing the person as you do so.

Black salt can be used in sachet powders, bottle spells, mojo bags and poppets.

Eggs

A raw egg (still in its shell) is a useful tool to take away illness, pain or disease. Roll the egg over the person who has the affliction; it draws out and contains the poison. The egg can then be taken and broken in a ritual to remove the affliction. It can be disposed of by throwing it to the ground at a crossroads, throwing it at a tree or into running water.

You can also use this method to 'draw out' negative feelings and energies from yourself or another. The egg traps them and can then be dispersed by disposing of the egg as mentioned above. Once the egg smashes the energy is harmlessly dispersed.

Cleaned ground egg shells can also be used as a powder for protection. This is referred to as Cascarilla powder and is generally used in Santeria practices. You can bake the shells in a low temperature oven for a few minutes after washing them to dry them out properly and make them easier to grind.

Use ground egg shells mixed with a little flour and hot water made into a paste to create chalk sticks.

Chalk Sticks

6 cleaned and dried egg shells ground to a fine powder

1 teaspoon of flour

1 teaspoon of hot water

Mix all the ingredients together and shape this into sticks by rolling small amounts onto a paper towel. Leave the sticks to dry for three days, then your egg shell chalk will be ready for use.

Poppets

Often called doll babies in Hoodoo, these usually represent a person. You might know them as Voodoo dolls, although I am not sure how much they are actually used in the religion of Voodou. You probably think of them as causing harm and death as well (thanks to Hollywood), but in actual fact poppets were originally used for healing and can be used for all sorts of intents both negative and positive. My research shows that poppets were used originally in ancient Egypt.

You can make a poppet out of anything: cloth, clay, twigs, corn husks, straw, wax or even a children's toy dolly.

Once you have made the basic 'person' shape (or purchased a dolly) you can dress it in colours or materials that represent the person the doll is intended to represent and add personal items such as hairs or nail clippings. Herbs can be stuffed inside or tucked into the fabric of its clothes; it can also be dressed with conjure oil.

The poppet can then be charged with your intent, whether it be healing, love, prosperity or otherwise. The poppet can be bound to another, buried, tended to, loved or, yes, you can even stick pins in it although the purpose of the pins can be to cause pain or to send healing to that particular area of the person's body.

Poppets can also be made in the image of Saints, Orishas or Loas, taking on their characteristics and placed on your altar.

Altars

An altar is your shrine or workspace that you set aside for your magical and spiritual practice. The area can be as simple or as decorative as you want it to be.

A Hoodoo altar may have a white, black or red cloth on it, sometimes a cross, usually candles and incense and then representations of deities – these could be statues or pictures of Orishas or saints depending on what faith you work with.

You can have as few or as many altars as you like, or have space for. You might just have one main working altar, but you may also have smaller ones for specific intents such as money, love and protection. Specific intent altars will have items that correspond with that intent.

A lot of Hoodoo practitioners will also have an ancestors altar. This will usually be covered in a white cloth and have candles, scents, bowls of water, incense and pictures of loved ones who have passed over, together with personal items such as jewellery. You can also add items that your ancestors were particularly fond of such as a glass of rum if they liked a drink or a small dish of tobacco if they liked to smoke.

Chapter 3

Laying Tricks

Laying tricks is a term used in Hoodoo and literally means working a spell by 'laying a trick' down such as powders, oils or herbs where the intended person will find it, walk over it or touch it. Within Hoodoo when you work a spell or perform a ritual it is often referred to as 'doing a job'. The 'job' might be as simple as dressing a candle or it might be a full-on ritual.

If you are working harmful tricks it is good practice to cleanse and protect yourself and your working area before and after creating the trick. I would also mention that if you do dish out harm, be mindful that people have the right to fight back…

Jinxes

To jinx means to curse, usually only by words or pointing. A jinx was originally when someone pointed a finger at you and shouted curses at you. These could be anything, such as, 'You are totally useless,' or, 'Everyone hates you.' These types of phrases are the ones that stick in your mind and worm their way into your self confidence and self esteem, they do the work from inside your head and heart.

The pointing of the finger adds power to the jinx; this can be taken a step further by using larger gestures such as pretending to shoot someone with your hand.

We use the word 'jinx' as well now when we talk about something before it happens, prompting someone to say, 'Don't jinx it,' by talking about it in case it brings the event bad luck.

Crossing and Uncrossing

If you feel you have been jinxed or cursed, what you really need to do first is to find out if you really have been. Get a reading from a reputable source, or do a reading for yourself either psychically or using divination.

If you have been going through a long run of bad luck then you may have been 'crossed' or jinxed.

Uncrossing can be done to remove the jinx. If you know the person who did it and how they did it that helps, but it is not necessary.

Have a look around your house and your property, see if you can find anything that has been disturbed and where someone might have buried a bottle (under your porch is a good place to start looking). If you find a package or bottle that is filled with herbs, powders and hair, burn it or dispose of it in running water.

If you don't find anything physical to get rid of, then you can work an uncrossing spell and you might also work a reversal spell to send the bad vibes back to the person who sent them to you.

It might also be worth cleansing and purifying your house and your body as well just to be on the safe side.

The addendum to this is also to ask yourself, 'Did I do something to hurt someone, who maybe I deserve this from? Would asking them to forgive me sort it out?' It's always worth considering!

Uncrossing candle spell

White candle (pillar or offertory)

Uncrossing oil (see the Oil chapter for the recipe)

Uncrossing powder (see the Powders chapter for the recipe)

Flame-proof dish or candle holder big enough to hold about a cup of water as well as the candle

Dress the candle with the oil and powder and stand it in the dish. Pour in about a cupful of blessed or spring water. Light the candle and say a blessing, chant or psalm over it; this works best if you say it three, seven or nine times. Let the candle burn out (it will go out once it hits the water level). Bury the candle stub at a crossroads and pour the water out there too, saying out loud a confirmation that you are now free from evil.

You can also use a reversing candle spell to uncross.

Reversing candle spell

Black or double action (black and white or black and red) candle
Uncrossing or reversing oil

Carve 'return to sender' on the spell candle or write a petition paper. Dress it with the oil. Light the candle and if possible place it on a mirror.

If it is a double action candle (a two-coloured candle), burn it to the centre then carve your name on the coloured or white end and your enemy's name on the black end. Dress your end with uncrossing oil and the other end with crossing oil. You can either burn one end and then turn it over and burn it from the other end or place the candle horizontally stuck in the centre with a nail (that has been nailed into a piece of wood first). This way both ends burn together although it does get a bit messy! This will reverse the spell and send it back to the person who set it in the first place.

Dispose of the stub by burying it at a crossroads or casting it into running water.

Empowering

Spells, herbs, candles, whatever a Hoodoo practitioner uses, will be empowered to add to their effectiveness. This can be done by prayers or blessings, visualising the desired outcome, invoking spirits to add their energy to it or sending energy into it. For any spell, trick, jinx or crossing to work I believe you need to be totally focused. To send energy you need to tap into the ashe or life force that the Earth and all natural things contain and direct this energy into your spell work.

Petition Papers

Petition papers and name papers are slips of paper that you write a person's name on, a symbol, sigil or short phrase corresponding with the intent of your spell work. Mostly the petition papers and name papers are placed under a candle, or added to a mojo bag or a bottle. Name papers will have a person's name on, the intended recipient of the spell, while a petition paper will have a wish or desire on it.

You can add to the oomph of the spell by using coloured ink to write on your paper, for instance black ink for protection and reversing spells, or green ink for money spells. In traditional Hoodoo only red or black ink would be used, and often it would be Dove's Blood, Dragon's Blood or Bat's Blood ink.

What paper you use is up to you, you can tear a small piece from a brown paper bag or a sheet of printer paper or you could use handmade parchment. Using paper with torn edges allows the magic to seep out. Use scissors for banishing petitions or for cutting ties with someone or something.

As a general guide for using petition papers you would write the person's name or your wish on the slip of paper three times, then turn the paper ninety degrees clockwise and write the name or wish again three times over the top of the first ones. The petition paper should then be dressed with a suitable oil blend.

The petition paper is then folded. To draw things to you the paper should be folded towards you, to banish something fold the paper away from you. Either way keep folding the paper until you can fold it no more.

The petition paper can then be placed under a candle, in a mojo bag or a bottle.

Coins

If you find a coin and it is laying heads up then it is considered to be a lucky coin, pick it up and use it in money drawing and prosperity spells. If you spot a coin and it is laying tails up then don't take it, it is considered to bring bad luck. You should, however, turn the coin over so that the next person to find it will have good luck. (Also see the section on coins in the chapter Miscellaneous Magic).

Chapter 4

Washes

Spiritual people have used washes as a way of cleansing both the body and the soul for centuries. These spiritual washes can be used in the bath or shower and also to wash the house, home and floors.

Again the Hoodoo washes are all based on conjure oil ingredients. The herbs and roots are steeped in water and then sieved, although a simpler method, but possibly not so traditional, is to use oil blends and add a few drops to water to wash the floors or add them to the bath to become a personal spiritual bath.

Floor washes are used for all sorts of purposes – mopping the floor to bring in good fortune and luck or to wash away negative energies and evil in the main. They can also be used for love, protection and healing etc.

There is a process to follow: when you want to clean your house in the spiritual, removing negative energy sense (and actually as a by-product in the physical sense) you start from the top of the building and work your way down, also working from the back of the house to the front, finishing up on your front doorstep.

To bring positive energy and prosperity into your home you should make sure your front doorstep is scrubbed clean, working inwards towards the home.

For ritual bathing of your own body, it works best if you wash yourself upwards to bring good fortune and downwards to dispel negativity.

Herbal baths work very well, using the magical properties of specific herbs to bring about the intent that you require. A lot of Hoodoo herbal bath mixes use magical numbers of herbs such as seven, nine or 13 different ingredients.

Any water that has been used for spiritual cleansing should be disposed of by throwing it away to the East, preferably before the sun rises. You don't have to lug bucketfuls of your used bathwater all the way outside to do this, you can use a small amount as a token.

Florida Water

Florida water is a scent that is used a lot in Hoodoo practice. It is generally used for cleansing. It can be used to wash your hands before magical or spiritual work, sprinkled around the home to cleanse negative energy, sprinkled on your altar, candles or any magical items or added to a bucket of water to wash your floors and work surfaces with.

It is called Florida water after the fountain of youth which was said to have been located in Florida.

Florida water usually has a base of citrus; this might be from sweet orange, lemon or neroli. It then often has lavender and clove added.

To make your own I encourage you to experiment to get a version that you like, but here are some ideas:

Florida Water Recipe

16oz distilled water
2oz alcohol (vodka works well, but it needs to be a high
    percentage proof)
6 drops bergamot essential oil
6 drops lavender essential oil
2 drops clove essential oil

Florida Water Recipe 2

4 cups alcohol (such as vodka)
½ cup lime juice (and the fruit itself)
½ cup lemon juice (and the fruit itself)
4 cloves

1 tablespoon dried lavender flowers

1 tablespoon dried vervain

Put the juices in a jar or bottle, chop up lemon and lime rind and add that into the jar. Add the cloves and herbs then finish off by pouring over the alcohol. Put a lid on the jar or bottle and leave it in a dark place for three to four weeks. Then strain the liquid into a clean bottle.

You could add any of the following suggested ingredients:

Ylang ylang

Lemon

Neroli

Mint

Bergamot

Cinnamon

Jasmine

Cloves

Lavender

Rose

Lime

Sweet orange

Vervain

Blue Water

Blue water is used for peace and protection, but also to dispel evil and negativity from a house.

Blue is the colour believed to be best at warding off evil and providing protection.

To make blue water use a glass and fill it with spring water or tap water with a teaspoon of salt added to it. To make it blue you can either use blue food colouring or laundry bluing (laundry bluing isn't so easily found in the UK). You can also add a drop or two of Florida water to it for added power. Charge the water with your intent, or draw a cross three times over the top of the glass to empower it, then leave the glass in a prominent place in your home. Change the water regularly.

Holy Waters

Often mentioned are the five or seven holy waters, they are made up of:

Holy water
Rain water
Spring water
River water
Ocean water

And to make it up to seven:

Florida water
Alcohol (usually whisky or rum)

These are mixed together – either the five or the seven to make a finished product. The water mixes can then be used sprinkled around the home for peace or to protect against negative energies.

Chinese Wash

Chinese Wash is a mainstay in Hoodoo practice and is used for removing negative energy, bad luck and evil, and bringing positive energy back in. The product originated sometime around the 1930s (possibly a bit earlier) and was marketed as Young's Chinese Wash. It was used for spiritual house cleaning, to purify the home and open up blockages allowing new beginnings, bringing good luck and peace to the home. The original recipe was a blend of oriental grasses with a citrus scent to it, similar to the ingredients used in Van Van Oil (see section on oils). Once purchased, Hoodoo practitioners then added a few pieces of straw from their household broom into the bottle. Chinese Wash can be purchased from retailers still. Some mixtures even have the broom straws already included, but you can also make it yourself.

The wash will need to be added to a bucket of water. Add a couple of teaspoons of the Chinese Wash mixture to make a floor wash.

Chinese Wash Recipe
Citronella

Lemongrass

Gingergrass

Palmarosa

Vertivert

A few straws from a besom

Liquid soap (castile)

A simplified version can be made by adding Van Van Oil to a liquid soap base.

Four Thieves Vinegar
Legend has it that during the Middle Ages a band of four thieves stole from the bodies of those who had died from the plague. They made a lot of money in the process, but never succumbed to the plague themselves. When they were eventually arrested they made a deal to share the secret of their protection from the illness in exchange for their lives. Their secret was a vinegar blend that they made and covered themselves in to ward against the plague.

Four Thieves Vinegar can be used for protection against illness, personal protection and banishing, and for cursing your enemies.

Most variations can be used topically and ingested, but always check the ingredients first because some that are for topical use contain herbs that may cause sickness or even be poisonous.

Recipes will vary but the base is… well… vinegar! You can use white vinegar, but cider or red wine vinegar works well. Add to your cider, red wine or white vinegar any or all of the following ingredients:

Garlic

Salt

Pepper – black or red

Basil

Sage

Lavender

Mint

Mustard seeds

Add your ingredients to the vinegar and put in a sealed bottle or jar; leave in a dark place for three or four weeks. You can then either leave all the herbs in the liquid or strain it into a new bottle.

This Four Thieves Vinegar can be taken internally – one teaspoon a day to protect against illness. You can also use it as a gargle for sore throats. Soak a cloth in the vinegar and inhale to clear your sinuses.

Add a couple of tablespoons of Four Thieves Vinegar to your bath water for protection.

To banish an enemy you would make up a bottle of Four Thieves Vinegar and then bury it under the victim's doorstep or porch, or you could even throw it at their porch so that the bottle smashes on their threshold.

To use it as a jinx against someone, use something personal from them such as a strand of hair or a photograph and put that into a bottle containing Four Thieves Vinegar, add nails and pins (nine of each works well), add a spoonful of graveyard dirt, shake the bottle and then bury it on their property.

Spiritual Body Cleansing

Once you have 'cleaned house' it is also important to spiritually cleanse your body to clear it of any negative energies. This is easily done using incense to smudge yourself or taking a cleansing bath.

To smudge your body use an incense mixture such as sandalwood, lavender, frankincense or myrrh. Smudge yourself with the smoke and say a cleansing prayer or blessing.

You can take a spiritual bath using essential oil blends added to your bath water or make up a cleansing bath salts mix.

Hand Washes

Herbal hand washes are mainly used for luck and prosperity. If you are a gambler, you tend to use your hands when throwing dice or using playing cards. You wash your hands in the herbal mixture just before you start your game for luck.

Lucky Hand Wash Recipe

2 tablespoons dried chamomile (or you could use a couple of chamomile teabags)

3 cups water

7 drops chamomile essential oil

Steep the chamomile teabags or dried chamomile in hot water for 10 minutes. Strain and then add the essential oil to the water. Store it in an airtight bottle or a spritzer. Pour a small amount into your palms and 'wash' your hands with it or using the spritzer to spray your hands to bring your gambling luck.

Bath Salts

Bath salt mixtures can be used in spiritual baths before spell work or a ritual. If you feel there is a blockage or illness within, you can use the bath salts to clear it.

Basic Bath Salts Blend

2 cups (16oz) salt crystals

1 cup (8oz) Epsom salts

¼ teaspoon of essential oil (your choice, pick one that corresponds with your intent, or use one of the oil blends in the Oils chapter).

Mix all the ingredients together. It can then be used straight away or kept in an airtight container for a few weeks.

I would suggest using a couple of tablespoons added to your bath water; you might need less or you might need a bit more depending on your bath size!

Soul Heal Bath Salts Recipe

2 cups (16oz) salt crystals

1 cup (8oz) Epsom salt

⅛ teaspoon peppermint essential oil

⅛ teaspoon lavender essential oil

Body Oils

Body oils can also be made and used to anoint your head and wrists or used on your full body as you would a body moisturiser. Please do a skin patch test before you go sloshing a whole load of body oil blend on, just in case you are allergic to any of the ingredients! (For information on the use of oils for tricks and spells, see the Oils chapter)

Body Oil Blend

16oz base oil such as sweet almond, grape seed or sunflower oil

1 teaspoon of essential oil – use a mixture of three or four oils that correspond to your intent

1 ½ cups dried herbs and/or roots

Place the herbs/roots in an airtight jar and pour over the base oil, store for four to six weeks, swirling the jar regularly. Then strain with a sieve and add your essential oil choices. Keep in an airtight jar and out of direct sunlight. Use as required.

Come To Me Body Oil

Base oil
Sweet orange essential oil
Lemon essential oil
Grated lemon peel
Add a piece of lodestone to the bottle

Blessing Body Oil

Base oil
Frankincense essential oil
Benzoin essential oil
Geranium essential oil
Rose petals

Body Powders

Body powders can be used instead of anointing with body oil. Make the body powder to the intention of the trick you will be working to add to its power.

Body Powder Blend

5 tablespoons arrowroot or cornstarch (corn flour)
2 tablespoons of baking soda
Herbs, roots, flowers of your choice (these will need to be ground to a fine powder) I would suggest in total about 3 tablespoons
½ teaspoon essential oil (mixture of your choice)

Add the oils to your ground herbs/root/flower mixture and mix, then add the arrowroot/cornstarch and baking soda

and blend together.
Store in an air tight jar.

Lift Me Up Body Powder Recipe

This is intended to refresh the spirit.

5 tablespoons cornstarch or arrowroot

2 tablespoons baking soda

1 tablespoon lavender

1 tablespoon ground orris root

1 tablespoon rose petals

¼ teaspoon palmarosa essential oil

¼ teaspoon violet oil

In Command Body Powder Recipe

This is to give you strength and control in any situation.

5 tablespoons corn starch or arrowroot

2 tablespoons baking soda

2 tablespoon marigold petals

1 tablespoon ground orris root

1 tablespoon lemon verbena

1 teaspoon dried orange peel

⅛ teaspoon frankincense essential oil

⅛ teaspoon myrrh essential oil

⅛ teaspoon vertivert essential oil

⅛ teaspoon sweet orange essential oil

Chapter 5

Oils

Oils are used a lot in Hoodoo, often called conjure oils, condition oils, anointing or dressing oils. And they all have fabulous names such as Van Van Oil, All Seeing Eye Oil and Bend Over Oil.

Originally Hoodoo practitioners would probably have used blessed olive oil (recipe below) to seal and dress candles, possibly because olive oil was available and was mentioned in the Bible.

The names are given to the oils to correspond with their use, the jinx they are meant for, the condition they are to cure etc. Money Draw Oil does what it says, Crossing Oil is used to cross someone, Bend Over Oil makes someone bend their will to yours and Van Van Oil is used to get rid of tricks, to bring luck and to disperse evil.

To use oil for anointing, you touch your finger into the oil and then put it on yourself or another person, leaving a drop of the oil on the skin. Dressing with oil means that you rub or drip oil onto an object such as a candle. *Note: be careful when anointing yourself or someone else with oil, test a small patch of the skin first to make sure there is no allergic reaction.*

Condition Oil is used in Hoodoo and is a name that groups together any anointing and dressing oils that are used against an unwanted condition or to bring something to you.

If you make your own oils then my advice is to use safe oils in both dressing and anointing blends. By safe I mean OK to use on your skin without you breaking out in a red blotchy rash – that way you can utilise all your oils for any purposes.

Oil Recipes

I have shared here some of the more popular oil blends, but for each one I have only made suggestions of ingredients to use.

Experiment with your own blends to create an oil that works for you. Traditional blends would have had set ingredients and I have included those, but have also added my own blends as well. Use a base oil such as almond oil with all of the recipes (except the blessed olive oil obviously!). Each ingredient stated in the recipes can be the essential oil or you can add in a small piece of the bark, plant or petal if you prefer. Alternatively you can use a base oil and add all the raw ingredients to 'steep' in the base oil, leave in a dark place for three to four weeks and your blend will be ready for use.

Blessed Olive Oil

Used a lot in Hoodoo this is a good all-round, all-purpose oil.

Use any variety of olive oil, although virgin or extra virgin oil is preferable as it is purer, and salt.

This process starts on a Sunday. Take a new bottle of olive oil and add a pinch of salt to it. You can then say a prayer or a blessing over the bottle. Re-seal the bottle and store it in a dark place. Then every day for a total of seven days repeat the process of adding a pinch of salt and saying a prayer or blessing. Once the process is complete you have a bottle of blessed olive oil ready to use.

Fast Luck Oil

Cinnamon (use the oil but you can also add a piece of cinnamon stick to the mixture too)
Vanilla
Wintergreen
Mint
Lemongrass

Fast Luck Oil is often coloured red using alkanet. The most commonly used ingredients for Fast Luck Oil are vanilla, winter-green and cinnamon. I have also seen recipes that include mint and lemongrass too, but cinnamon is always the base used.

Money Draw Oil

Frankincense

Sandalwood

Myrrh

Bayberry (root or leaf)

Cedar

Pyrite chips are often added to Money Draw Oil.

Come To Me Oil

Rose

Patchouli

Vanilla

Add one or a pair of lodestones to charge the oil

Uncrossing Oil

Lemon

Bay

Rose

Lily

King Solomon Wisdom Oil

For wisdom and psychic abilities.

Solomon Seal

Hyssop

Rose

Altar Oil

For blessing yourself or objects for your altar.

Frankincense

Myrrh
Cedar

Confusion Oil

To create confusion in your enemy.

Marjoram
Patchouli
Poppy seeds
Mustard seeds

Bend Over Oil

To bend the will of another to your own, make others do your bidding.

Frankincense
Rose
Liquorice
Bergamot

Abramelin Oil

This is a ritual oil described in a medieval grimoire *The Book of the Sacred Magic of Abramelin the Mage*, a Jewish Kabbalist. The ingredients are cinnamon for luck, prosperity, success and money; calamus or galangal is used for control over others; myrrh is for the Lord and olive oil is for stability and grounding. It is particularly useful for court cases.

4 parts cinnamon bark (ground)
2 parts myrrh resin (ground)
1 part galangal root (ground) or calamus root (ground)
Olive oil – weigh the ground ingredients and then add half
  the weight in olive oil

Van Van

Van Van is probably the most well known name in Hoodoo for oils, incense and powders. Van Van dispels evil, negative energies, gives protection, changes bad luck and opens the way for new beginnings.

Van Van is taken from a French word 'verveine' which is the plant verbena (sometimes called vervain).

Van Van Oil Recipe

Sweet almond carrier oil then add a mixture of the following ingredients (I have seen many variations of recipes for Van Van Oil so I would encourage you to experiment with blends and go with what works for you):

Lemongrass
Verbena (vervain)
Sweet grass
Five finger grass
Citronella
Palmarosa
Gingergrass
A pinch of blessed salt, magnetic sand and/or a lodestone can also be added.

Chapter 6

Incense

Incense is used in Hoodoo as it is in most magical practices. Most of the incenses derive from the conjure oils and use the same ingredients. Colouring is often added to the incense as well to correspond with the intent. Loose incense is most commonly used within Hoodoo.

A lot of Hoodoo incenses are very basic and use tree resins, herbs and woods that when burnt give off a pleasing scented smoke. Sage and tobacco are often used along with sandalwood, frankincense, myrrh, pine and copal.

I have included some recipes below. They are my own recipes based on traditional Hoodoo ones. All of them are for loose incense to be burnt on charcoal discs. The recipes include suggested ingredients, experiment with your own blends!

Uncrossing Incense
Dragon's Blood
Powdered eggshell
Salt
Sage

Fast Luck Incense
Cinnamon
Cedar
High John the Conqueror root (ground)

Purification Incense
Sage
Frankincense
Myrrh

Rosemary
Salt

Seven Powers of Africa Incense

Frankincense
Myrrh
Cinnamon
Sage
Sandalwood
Dragon's Blood

Money Draw Incense

Nutmeg
Cinnamon
Sandalwood
Cedar

Love Draw Incense

Cinnamon
Rose
Lilac
Honey

Un-Jinx Incense

Cloves
Garlic
Copal
Dragon's Blood

Chapter 7

Mojo Bags

Let's forget the media version of what 'mojo' means, it isn't anything to do with the male sexual organ!

The word mojo seems to have come from the West African word 'mojuba', which means prayer or praise, so your mojo bag is a bag containing a prayer, a wish bag if you like.

You might also see the mojo bag referred to as a gris-gris, which means charm or fetish. It may also be called a conjure hand, conjure bag, trick bag or root bag.

Traditionally a mojo bag is made from red flannel and is sometimes referred to as a 'flannel'. However, I often like to use different coloured felts to match the colour to the intent of the bag. Objects are placed into the bag that are relevant to the intent and all contain strong ashe. These materials might be graveyard dirt, nails, ground bones, sticks, stones, roots, small bones, herbs, minerals – whatever the practitioner believes should go in to work the trick correctly.

Once the bag is filled it is dressed with conjure oil and tied up, and will then be 'fed' regularly with powder, oil or alcohol.

A mojo bag is 'alive' with energy and must be fed to keep the ashe working. The feeding adds magic and energy to the trick to keep its life force going. Often the feeding corresponds with specific days of the week that are connected with particular Orishas, saints or deities. I have included some 'feeding powder' recipes below. You can use these on a regular basis to feed your mojo bag; just take a pinch and sprinkle it into the bag and say a prayer or blessing as you do so to 'recharge' the energy. You can also use one of the oil blends to feed your mojo bag instead of the powder, but only add a few drops at a time otherwise you will end up with a very soggy mojo bag!

A mojo bag has many, many different uses from fast luck to unhexing.

Obviously slaves would not have had access to such things as crystals, but I have added them to the mojo bag recipes here because I believe this adds to their power; you don't have to include them in your bags if don't wish to.

Unhex Mojo Bag

Red, purple or black flannel

Cord to tie it up with

A piece of High John the Conqueror root

1 piece of agate crystal

Pinch of St John's wort

A piece of rosemary

Feeding Powder

Hyssop

Rosemary

Angelica root

Rose essential oil

Frankincense essential oil

Grind all the ingredients together to make a fine powder.

Money Draw Mojo Bag

Red or green flannel

Cord to tie it up with

Cloves (whole)

Allspice (whole)

A feather

1 piece of peridot or malachite

A piece of High John the Conqueror root

A whole nutmeg

Mint

Feeding Powder

High John the Conqueror root
Cloves
Chamomile essential oil

Grind all the ingredients together to make a fine powder.

Peace Mojo Bag

Red, white or light blue flannel
Cord to tie it up with
Myrrh
Frankincense
Angelica root
An amethyst crystal
Van Van Oil
Salt
Tobacco

Feeding Powder

Lavender flowers
Angelica root
Lavender essential oil
Sage

Grind all the ingredients together to make a fine powder.

Health and Healing Mojo Bag

Red or blue flannel
Cord to tie it up with
Rosemary
Lemon balm
A quartz crystal
Salt
Frankincense

Feeding Powder

Rosemary
Sage
Salt
Frankincense essential oil

Grind all the ingredients together to make a fine powder.

Warding Mojo Bag

Black or purple flannel
Cord to tie it up with
Vervain
Lemon grass
Sweet grass
Tobacco

Feeding Powder

Van Van Oil
Sage
Tobacco

Grind all the ingredients together to make a fine powder.

Nation Sacks

A variation on the mojo bag is a nation sack. Sorry guys this one is just for the ladies. Originally it was used by women to dominate their man or to keep him faithful, loving and generous.

Traditionally the 'sack' is a small pouch made from red flannel. It is then filled with roots, herbs, minerals and sometimes bodily fluids all with the intent of keeping the woman strong and keeping her man in line. The sack is then tied with cord and kept about the woman's person, and must never be touched by a man!

Chapter 8

Bottle Spells

I use bottle spells a lot. I always have what I refer to as witch bottles in my home for protection and 'soaking up' any negative energies.

A bottle spell is just that... a spell in a bottle. You can use just a plain, cleaned jam jar with a lid or a used vinegar bottle; you could use pretty glass bottles purchased from craft or charity stores. Old medicine bottles work well too.

Witch bottles were originally buried in walls and chimneys of households to ward off evil and witches. (Thankfully they aren't generally used for that now, although there are still areas of the globe where people believe witches to be evil.) Old witch bottles dating back centuries have been found to have contained nails, urine, hair, broken glass and nail clippings.

Charm Flasks

Charm flasks are found mainly in Latin America and are flasks or bottles that contain charms used for luck or protection along with magical herbs and oils. Some of them also contain Catholic symbols and sigils. Once filled, the flask will be blessed and a prayer said. It is then left on the altar for the duration of the spell.

Vinegar Bottles

Bottle spells that are filled with vinegar are used with the purpose of souring a relationship between two people.

Break Up Bottles

A break up bottle does pretty much what it says on the label – it is used to separate people. Usually the bottle includes a hair from a dog and one from a cat (preferably black), encouraging the recipients of the trick to fight like cats and dogs. Added to that are nine coffin nails, nine pins and nine needles all with the intent that they cause harm to each other. Peppercorns can be added to cause anger and then you can add your own choice of ingredients such as sachet powders or graveyard dirt. Bodily fluids can be added to help connect the bottle to a certain person. Be careful with vinegar sealed in a bottle though because if left for a very long time it has a tendency to explode!

Once you have filled your jar you need to lay the trick by throwing it at a crossroads, into running water, burying it under the victim's doorstep or throwing it on their property.

Hot Foot Jars

These bottle/jar spells work with hot foot magic by driving away your enemies or any troublesome people. Use a clean jar or even better use an empty hot, spicy sauce bottle. Write the name of your enemy on a name paper, but write the name backwards seven, nine or 13 times (your choice, go with what feels best). Put the paper in the bottle. Then add hot foot powder to the bottle and shake it, calling out a curse to send the person on their way. Do this each day until the trick has worked then throw the bottle away in running water.

Honey Jar Spells

This is a very traditional type of bottle spell. It is basically a jar or even a box that has a sweet liquid inside, you then add your magical ingredients, such as connections to the person if you are directing it towards a particular individual, herbs and maybe a written charm on a piece of paper. This is all topped off by dressing a candle with a corresponding conjure oil and then the candle is burnt on top of the jar. You can use honey as the sweet liquid or you can use granulated or cubed sugar as well just as effectively, but if you use granulated or cubed sugar you might want to dissolve it in water first to make a syrup.

A Honey Jar Spell to Sweeten a Person

If there is a person who needs their personality sweetened, or you want to make them like you more, or you perhaps want a raise in your job and need to 'sweeten up' your boss, this is the trick to work.

What you need:

A jar with a metal lid
Honey, syrup or sugar
Slip of paper and a pencil
Personal items such as hair or nail clippings
A candle
Dressing oil

Fill your jar with your chosen sweetener. Then write the person's name on the slip of paper; write it out three times, each time on a separate line. Then turn the slip of paper around clockwise a quarter turn and write your own name three times, each time on a separate line.

What you should have now is your names crossing each other.

On the space around the names, write down your wish; be specific. Write it around the edge of the paper so that it forms a circle around the names. This needs to be written without taking your pencil or pen off the paper and needs to be written in a continuous flow without any spaces. Make sure you join up the first and last words so that they form a circle. When you have done that you can go back and dot any 'i's and cross any 't's if you wish.

Once that is done fold the paper towards you and then speak your wish out loud. Turn the paper and fold it again, keep doing this – turning and folding towards you – to bring your wish to you until you can't fold it any more.

If you want to add herbs or personal items to the trick, add them inside the piece of paper before you fold it, you could add rose petals for love, a clove for friendship or a piece of hair. Be creative and go with what feels right for you.

When you are ready, you will need to eat three spoonfuls of the honey, syrup or sugar. As you eat each one, state your wish out loud.

Then put the folded piece of paper into the jar and close the lid.

Next dress your candle with conjure oil (see the chapter on oils for recipe ideas). You can also correspond the colour of your candle with the intent of your working. Then put the candle on top of the jar lid. You might need to pop a few drops of melted candle wax on the lid first to fix the candle in place.

Light the candle and let it burn fully. You don't have to burn it all in one go, but make sure you eventually burn it right out. Burn it on a Monday, Wednesday and Friday until it is done. You can keep this trick working by adding a new candle to the lid each time one burns right out until your desire is fulfilled.

The honey jar spell will work very well without the addition of a candle, but I find it adds more oomph to the trick and gets things working faster and is more powerful in the long run, but it is a personal choice.

Painted Bottle Spells

I have seen some beautifully painted bottles that are essentially witch bottles with specific intents. The bottles are painted in corresponding colours to the intent with pretty images on the front, so a money draw bottle would be painted green with gold dollar or pound signs painted on the front and a love spell bottle might be painted pink with hearts painted on the front. These bottles can be reused as they usually contain written petitions along with herbs and minerals. Corresponding candles can be burnt on top of the bottle as in the honey jar spell or alongside it.

You will also find painted bottle spells with a religious theme, often painted with images of patron saints or Orishas on the front. Herbs and minerals are popped into the bottle and then a prayer written on a slip of paper is put into the top of the bottle. A candle is added to the top and dressed with oil, then lit.

Shaking Bottle Spells

Shaking a bottle spell once you have laid the trick gives it a bit of a stir up, gets the energy within the spell working, adds extra oomph to it. If you keep the bottle spell for an ongoing trick you can regularly shake it to keep it going.

War Water Bottles

A Hoodoo War Water bottle would be sent, left on your doorstep or thrown at an enemy. Each bottle contained, basically, a swampy or bloody yuck, which if thrown at your property would smash and leave a foul smelling mess. It has been said that to break a bottle of War Water on the property of your enemy will bring strife and sorrow to their household; I would imagine that just the mess would be enough!

War Water bottles may have contained such items as black feathers, blood (probably from chickens) or if you were squeamish possibly a blood substitute (beetroot or tomato juice for instance), moss, rusty nails and broken glass among other things. Magnetic sand, moss and rusty water were often added too.

Each item is symbolic – the nails were to tie down wayward spirits and broken glass suggested the transparent spirit world and they all came together to give the warning.

Peace Water Bottles

On the flipside of War Water is Peace Water; bottles filled with Peace Water are used to bring well... peace to the home. They also encourage friendly visitors and positive energy together with protection for your house. Peace Water is usually made from two blue liquids and a clear one (one of them being an oil so that they separate), each one has different herbal scents. I have also seen Peace Water as two liquids, one clear and one blue. When the bottle is left to stand, the layers separate. To use it, you shake the bottle and, walking backwards, sprinkle droplets of the Peace Water in each corner of each room in your home.

I think the story behind Peace Water is the saying 'to pour oil over troubled waters' meaning to soothe and calm the spirits.

Chapter 9

Foot Track Magic

Feet are important right? Without them we wouldn't get very far, our feet also connect us to the Earth. In Hoodoo the belief is that where you walk you leave footprints, spiritual ones. A good Hoodoo practitioner will know where she walks and her daily routine. Another Hoodoo practitioner wishing to cause harm will seek out that path and take advantage of it, placing magical obstructions in his or her way.

Hot Foot Powder

One of the most well known foot track magic powders is Hot Foot Powder. The usual ingredients are hot chillies, sulphur, cayenne pepper, black pepper and any powder that is hot or irritating.

Hot Foot Powder is sprinkled on the ground where your intended victim will walk over it. Once that person has stepped into it, that powder will be carried with them into their home or car, taking the magic into their lives. It can be used to drive away unwanted people, make enemies leave or basically make people you don't like get out of your life!

To make your own powder you can use:

Cayenne pepper
Graveyard dirt
Chilli powder
Black pepper
Sulphur

I also use Hot Foot Powder sprinkled around the boundaries of my home to keep out unwanted visitors and to protect my house.

For more on powders, see the following chapter.

Chapter 10

Powders

Powders are used a lot in Hoodoo, sprinkling powders, blowing powders and feeding powders. Sprinkling and blowing powders are usually called 'sachet powders'.

They can be used to purify and protect a room, your home and your property. They can also be used to bring things to you such as money, happiness and love. They can also be sprinkled on another's property to set a jinx in place. And they are used in mojo bags to feed the ashe.

There are a basic set of ingredients used in the powders such as sugar, magnetic sand, salt, graveyard dirt, cayenne pepper, black pepper and sulphur. Talcum powder is often added too.

The naming of sachet powders works on the same principle as the oils – the names derive from the intent and purpose of the trick.

Blowing sachet powders involves blowing (that was obvious wasn't it?) the powder towards a person or their representation (a photo for instance) or blowing the powder to the four directions – North, East, South and West to bring good and positive energy.

Sprinkling sachet powders is often done by walking backwards using foot track magic. Taking 21 steps you walk backwards, bent over, sprinkling the powder as you go. Twenty-one steps are important because it is three times seven, but you can use any variation of steps as long as it uses three, seven or nine – all magical numbers. You might like to also say a chant or state your desire as you sprinkle the powder too.

You can also use conjure powders for laying down tricks, which involves using the powder to make different patterns or sigils. This can be done on the ground for the intended person to walk through or across. It can also be done on your altar when you are working with a candle spell or within ritual. Your candles can also be dressed with the powder; dress it first with oil and then add the powder for extra oomph.

Powders can also be used to dress your hands. Start by cleansing your hands, soap and water will do, but a dowsing in Florida Water or alcohol works best, then allow them to dry in the air. Next rub your hands together to create a feeling of heat. Put a pinch of your chosen powder onto your hands and then rub them together to evenly distribute the powder. Then using the first two fingers of your right hand make an 'X' sign on your left palm (you can also quote a prayer or blessing at this point). Spit on your hands and rub them together. This is very useful if you like to gamble!

Powders can be sprinkled onto paperwork for tests and applications along with love letters – use your imagination and the ideas are limitless!

If you use natural and safe ingredients in your powders you can also use them on your body too.

Sachet Powder Recipes

For all these recipes use talcum powder or cornstarch (corn flour) as a base, then add the other ingredients to it. Use quantities that seem right to you; grind all the ingredients in a pestle and mortar until they form a powder. Again these recipes are my own blends based on traditional Hoodoo ideas.

Money Draw Powder

Frankincense
Magnetic sand
Basil
Poppy seeds
Cinnamon

Come To Me Powder

Sandalwood
Myrtle
Frankincense
Rose oil

Bend Over Powder

Frankincense
Liquorice root
Rose
Bergamot

Lucky Powder

Nutmeg
Allspice
Basil
Vertivert oil

Blessing Powder

Lavender
Ylang Ylang
Musk

Confusion Powder

Coconut
Lavender
Black pepper
Violet

Happiness Powder

Lavender
Catnip
Marjoram

Healing Powder

Eucalyptus
Thyme
Carnation
Myrrh

Cast Off Evil Powder

Bay
Black pepper
Salt
Garlic
Chilli pepper

High John the Conqueror Powder

This is used for luck, money draw and sexual power.

High John the Conqueror root
Rose petals
Magnetic sand
Palmarosa oil

Queen Elizabeth Powder

This is used for love.

Queen Elizabeth root
Arrowroot
Lavender flowers
Violet petals

Love Drawing Powder

Sandalwood
Cinnamon
Basil
Frankincense
Rose

Sprinkling Salts

This is a type of sachet powder that uses salt in the mix instead of the talcum powder or cornstarch. Use them in the same way you would sachet powders (although it is probably not a good idea to use them on your skin). The salt can also be dyed using food colouring to correspond with the intent. Add ground herbs, roots and oils to the salt base.

Goofer Dust

Goofer is a Kikongo word (kufwa) that means 'to die' or 'to kill' – this stuff ain't for the faint hearted. Goofer dust is used to cause harm and illness, but can also be used to create domination over a loved one. Be under no illusions, as far as I am aware goofer dust is only ever used to cause harm.

Some of the ingredients you can use in goofer dust are graveyard dirt, dried ground snakeskin, sulphur, salt, ash, ground bones, powdered insects, herbs (mullein works well), spices, black or red pepper, magnetic sand and dried manure.

Goofer dust is used in much the same way as hot foot powder; it is foot track magic. Sprinkle the powder in the path of an enemy. The goofer dust is then taken up through their feet to do its work. Again, as with all powders, it can also be utilised by sprinkling on the victim's clothes or bedding or added to a mojo bag or bottle and buried on their property.

Laying a trick with this powder is referred to as having 'goofered' someone i.e. cursed.

Using goofer dust in a love spell will cause the intended person pain and suffering in order to force them to submit to the will of the person laying the trick on them. This interferes with the free will of any person.

To counteract or reverse a goofering you can use spiritual washes, candle spells and uncrossing rituals.

Chapter 11

Candle Magic

Candles are used a lot in Hoodoo, in fact there is pretty much a candle for every situation! Votive candles are generally used in devotion to spirits and saints, tea lights are used while taking a spiritual bath, pillar candles are used for long-term laying of tricks. Shaped candles are used a lot for specific intents.

I believe that originally any spells or Hoodoo magic would have been performed using oil lamps, but also basic white candles would have been available. However, I have included a colour guide here as modern Hoodoo practice seems to use colour magic.

Colours

Colour symbolism is used a lot with Hoodoo candles. As a general rule go with your instincts, but here is a guide:

White: Blessings, spiritual, protection, cleansing and passing over – white can also be used as a good substitute if you don't have coloured candles.

Black: Banishing, dispelling negativity, curses and removing unwanted people.

Grey: To stop a spell, to neutralise a situation, sleep and storm magic.

Red: Love, lust, passion, sex, anger, heat and protection.

Pink: Love, friendship and feminine energy.

Orange: Luck, new opportunities, success and wishes.

Green: Money, growth, prosperity, luck and nature.

Yellow: Clarity, communication, wisdom, happiness and cleansing.

Purple: Psychic ability, power, influence, control, domination and success.

Blue: Peace, protection from evil and healing.

Brown: Stability, grounding, legal matters, to prevent change.

Gold: Masculine energy, fame, success, glamour and wealth.

Silver: Feminine energy, protection and wealth.

Hoodoo Candles or Seven-Day Glass Candles

These are pillar candles encased in a glass jar; they have specific colours and correspondences and often have a picture on the front that shows the intent of that candle.

To fix a Hoodoo candle with your intent start by writing a petition on a slip of paper, then charge the candle with your intent. Next, make three or five holes in the top of the candle with a nail or a screwdriver about an inch or so in depth. Then drop some conjure oil into the holes you have just made. You can also sprinkle some powder or herbs on the top of the candle at this point if you wish.

Seal your intent in the candle by tapping it three times and saying your intent out loud, then place the candle on top of your slip of paper. Light the candle and say your intent once more. Allow the candle to burn for as long as you are able to keep watch over it, then snuff it out (don't blow it, just pinch the wick between wet fingers) and do the same process again the next day, feeding it again with a little conjure oil and lighting the candle, allowing it to burn again for as long as you are able to. When the candle has finally burnt down completely the spell is complete.

Seven-day candles can also incorporate calling upon the seven powers. During the candle spell you call upon Eleggua to remove all obstacles, Chango for power over your enemies, Obatula for peace, Ogum for work, Orula to open doors, Oshun to bring love and Yemaya to bring abundance.

Seven-Knob Candles

The seven-knob or wishing candle is usually found in the form of seven balls stacked on top of one another, the idea being that each knob has a different intent or you can use the same intent seven times just with added oomph. If you can't find a readymade knob candle you can use a pillar or taper candle and mark out seven sections to it. You can carve a phrase or a symbol into each section and dress it with conjure oil. Sprinkle with some sachet powder too if you want. Light the candle and say your intent out loud, snuff the flame by pinching with wet fingers when the first section has burnt down, repeat each day for seven days. Bury the remains.

Altar Candles

Sometimes called invocation candles, these are used on the altar for spiritual worship. They are often large candles and set higher than any others on your altar. An altar candle should be lit at the beginning of any work or ritual and be the last one snuffed out when your work is finished. They are traditionally white in colour and often dressed in an altar oil. Although you can also use smaller, coloured candles for your altar if you wish.

Break-Up Candles

Break up candles are used in Hoodoo and are often in the shape of a naked man and woman standing back to back, sometimes on a heart. The candles are usually black in colour. They are used to aid in the break up or separation of a couple.

You carve the name of each person on the candle or even pin a photograph to each one. Dress the candle in a suitable oil such as break-up or crossing oil then light the candle. If you have a photograph of the couple together you could also tear the photo in half as well. If the design of candle allows, you could also cut the candle down the centre to separate the figures.

Once the candle has burned down, wrap the remains in two separate cloths and dispose of them at a crossroads as far apart from each other as is possible.

Lovers' Candles

These candles are usually in the form of two naked figures entwined and are often red or pink in colour. They can be used in sex, love or lust spells to bring about passion, romance and sex.

Reversing Candles

Reversing candles do what it says... they reverse things. The candles themselves are usually red inside with an outer coating of black wax. As the candle burns the black wax disappears leaving the red wax inside, thus symbolising the evil being burnt away. They can also be half and half, as in one half of the candle is black and the other half is white or red or green depending on the condition that needs to be reversed. They can be turned upside down or burnt at both ends to reverse or undo tricks.

Triple Action Candles

Traditionally red, white and blue or red, white and green, these candles are three colours and are burnt over the course of three days, one colour section each day.

Carve a symbol into each section of the candle, for instance a pound or dollar sign for money, a heart for love etc, dress the candle with conjure oil, write your petition on a slip of paper and stand the candle on top of it, charge with your intent then light the candle. Once the first section of the candle has burnt down snuff the flame by pinching it with wet fingers (don't blow it out as that disturbs the energy of the spell). The following day charge the candle again and relight it, burn that section then snuff the flame. On the third day charge the candle with your intent again then relight. Let this last section burn out naturally.

Triple action candles can be used for three different intents all in one candle, so the red section is for matters of the heart, the white section for peace or protection and the green section for drawing money.

Religious or Vigil Candles

Similar to Hoodoo candles in that they are pillar candles set in glass jars, these have labels or pictures on the front of the saints and often the Virgin Mary or Jesus. They also often have prayers printed on the back of the candle jar. These candles can be burnt as petitions to the saints. Fix these candles in a similar way to that of the Hoodoo candles before burning. You can also find these glass encased candles with pictures of the planets and the zodiac signs on too.

Offertory Candles

These are straight sided candles usually about six inches in height, sometimes called 'household' candles. They are useful for inscribing and dressing to use for prayer, spiritual and magical purposes.

Loading Candles

This term really just means putting things on the candle i.e. loading it up. Items used can be conjure oils, powders, herbs, ground roots, crystals, minerals, and personal items such as hair or nail clippings.

I often just load a candle by dressing the top with conjure oil and sprinkling on a few corresponding herbs, but if you want to really go for it you can load the candle by turning it upside down and hollowing out a section in the base (works best with pillar candles otherwise it is too fiddly) then fill the cavity you have made with your oils, herbs, powders or whatever you want to use, then take another lit candle and drip wax over the hole to seal all the goodies inside.

Chapter 12

Lamp Magic

Before the advent of electricity a lot of homes would use oil lamps, these can be used within Hoodoo magic. Herbs, roots and a drop or two of conjure oil can be added to the reservoir of the lamp. You can also drop in small crystals or minerals too, although crystals are not traditional. Personalise the lamp to the intent of the spell you wish to work. I would suggest that when adding conjure oils to the reservoir, you keep to natural oils, nothing that will cause an explosion or toxic gases!

Petition or name papers can then be added, prepared in the usual manner and pinned to the wick of the oil lamp.

You don't even need to use a readymade oil lamp, they can easily be made from coffee tins, hurricane lamps or even natural items such as a coconut shell.

Money Drawing Lamp Spell

A stick of cinnamon
Sassafras root
Ginseng
Lodestone
Pyrite
Four silver coins
Small amount of honey
Slip of paper
Personal items, such as a few strands of hair

Write your name on the slip of paper three times, turn it 90 degrees and write your name again three times. Dress the paper with honey and add a few drops of an oil blend such as Money Draw Oil. Place a couple of strands of your hair onto the paper, and then pin the name paper to the wick of your lamp.

Add the other items, the coins and herbs etc, to the lamp reservoir, pop a few drops of Money Draw Oil on top.

Fill the reservoir of the lamp with lamp oil.

Light the wick and say a prayer or a blessing over it while it burns. Visualise your required end result.

Keep working with this until you get the desired result.

Chapter 13

Sigils and Symbols

Sigils, symbols and names are often carved into candles to add to the intent, power and purpose of the spell.

To draw something to you carve your symbol or sigil into the candle by starting from the bottom and make your sigil 'grow' moving it upwards. To banish something start your carving from the top of the candle moving downwards.

If you are drawing letters you can stack them, by drawing each letter one over the top of another. Again if you are drawing something to you start to carve at the bottom of the candle and if you are banishing something start at the top.

The spiral method means you start your carving at the bottom of the candle and move to the right, spiralling the letters of your carving upwards to bring something towards you, or start at the top and spiral downwards to banish something.

For a straightforward carving just draw your design in the middle of the candle, it could be a heart for a love spell or a pound/dollar sign to draw money.

To reverse a spell or when banishing negativity, you could try writing a word backwards on the candle.

If you don't want anyone to see what you have carved into the candle use a needle as this makes a very fine line and even you probably won't be able to make out the end result, but the important thing is that spirit will.

Another way of hiding what you are doing is by carving your intent on the base of the candle so that no one can see it.

Chapter 14

Crossroads Magic

A place where two roads cross has always been a magical location. It is a useful place for leaving offerings, burying spells or candle stubs and is thought to be where the worlds meet; a place of spirits.

You can make your own crossroads if you aren't near one and need it for your spell or laying tricks. You can draw with chalk or sprinkle an outline with powder or salt to make a circle with a cross inside. You can draw it on the ground or on your altar. This is commonly referred to as a 'cross mark'. If you need to be a bit more discreet you can just mark dots where the lines would touch the edge of the outer circle and a centre spot, this is referred to as a 'five spot'. This is also sometimes called a quincunx or a cosmogram.

The five spot is generally used for sealing and fixing spells in place. You place items at each of the five spots; what you put there depends on location and the type of spell. Items used might be graveyard dirt, sachet powders, salt or powdered minerals.

If you can access the floorboards in a room, this is much preferred. Then you can fix the trick by laying five bundles of ingredients, such as roots, personal items, herbs, stones etc, literally under the floorboards at the five spots. You could also use thick rugs or items of furniture within the house to hide the bundles under.

If you have fitted carpets on the floors you could use spiritual waters to mark the five spots, but any liquid is considered a temporary measure as it evaporates and will need to be renewed.

You can also fix a protection trick by using four spot points outside your property, one at each corner. This makes it easier for burying bundles of ingredients. The centre point can be more discreet as it will be inside the house and is quite often salt.

Candle spells often incorporate the five spot method. Sachet powders are used at the four outer points and items from the spell left in the centre while the candle spell burns.

Crossroads are an excellent place for crossroad rituals (or spells) and also a good place to dispose of used spell remnants. To dispose of an item at the crossroads, throw it over your left shoulder towards the middle of the crossroads and walk away, never look back.

Candle wax stubs, ashes and leftover sachet powders are also good items to dispose of at a crossroads, especially if the items have been used in jinxes or harmful tricks.

Chapter 15

Miscellaneous Magic

Prayers and Blessings

A lot of Hoodoo spells require a prayer or blessing to be said while working the trick. You can use whatever words resonate with you, you can use chants that you know or you can make up your own. I personally tend to invoke an Orisha that is suitable for the intent and say some words as a request, but The Lord's Prayer and Psalm 23 here are commonly used by Hoodoo practitioners who work with Christianity.

Psalm 23

The Lord is my shepherd; I shall not want.

He maketh me to lie down in green pastures: he leadeth me beside the still waters.

He restoreth my soul: he leadeth me in the paths of righteousness for his name's sake.

Yea, though I walk through the valley of the shadow of death, I will fear no evil: for thou art with me; thy rod and thy staff they comfort me.

Thou preparest a table before me in the presence of mine enemies: thou anointest my head with oil; my cup runneth over.

Surely goodness and mercy shall follow me all the days of my life: and I will dwell in the house of the Lord forever.

The Lord's Prayer

Our Father which art in heaven, Hallowed be thy name.

Thy kingdom come, Thy will be done in Earth, as it is in Heaven.

Give us this day our daily bread.

And forgive us our debts, as we forgive our debtors.

And lead us not into temptation, but deliver us from evil: For thine is the kingdom, and the power, and the glory, forever.

Amen

It is personal choice as to what you say and whether you use these or your own.

Moon Phases

Many root workers will align their spell working with the phases of the moon. Spells that draw things to you, attract things or bring positive things to you will be worked or at least started when the moon is in her waxing phase. Spells that are worked to banish something or end things, break up spells and foot track magic are started or worked fully when the moon is waning. Root workers may also align their spell working with the zodiac and/or the corresponding days of the week. I am not sure how traditional the use of moon phases is within Hoodoo, but I have found that it works for me.

Divination

Divination is used by some root workers, but usually in the form of cards or tea leaves. Tarot cards may be used, but also a normal set of playing cards. One of the oldest types of Hoodoo divination is 'throwing the bones'. The items 'thrown' are animal bones, quite often chicken, snake or possum bones. Each bone will have its own meaning and how it falls will add to the meaning of the reading. Dream divination is also used in Hoodoo.

Cold Box Spells

Your own fridge or freezer can be utilised for binding spells, to stop someone doing something, to stop a situation, or to literally freeze someone in their tracks. They can also be used for stopping gossip.

You will need a container such as a box or even an envelope; you can also use fruit or vegetables that are symbolic to the situation. Write the name on a slip of paper of the person or situation you wish to freeze or stop, dip the paper in plain water or spiritual water (to help it freeze) then tuck it into the container you are going to use. Make sure the container is securely sealed. Place the container in the freezer or your ice box; leave it there until the situation is resolved.

Chalk Marks

Marks and sigils are often drawn on the ground within Hoodoo and the most commonly used ways to do this are chalk and talcum-based powders. Quite often these chalk marks are used for protection or in crossing magic. Once drawn, the practitioner will spit on the chalk design to activate the power. Crossing marks are used so that the intended person steps over them or across them, as they do so the magic kicks into action.

If you realise that someone has laid crossing marks against you, the best way to counteract them is simply to sweep them away with a broom. If you feel the magic is particularly strong and the sweeping hasn't done the trick you can also draw over the pattern yourself with a mixture of salt and sulphur, this works as an anti-jinx. You might also want to wash the area with a spiritual wash too.

Coins

Coins are used a lot in Hoodoo for spells that involve bringing money or drawing money to you. The coins used are usually silver. They are also used a lot in spells for gamblers to bring them good luck and fortune. If you find a coin and it is laying heads up then it is considered to be a lucky coin, pick it up and use it in money drawing and prosperity spells. If you spot a coin and it is laying tails up then don't take it, it is considered to bring bad luck. You should, however, turn the coin over so that the next person to find it will have good luck.

Chapter 16

Disposing of Tricks

Any trick or spell involves the use of energy or ashe. Each of the ingredients used, whether it is roots, herbs or powders, carries that energy with it. So once you are done with laying down a trick and you have remnants left over it is important to dispose of them properly.

Burning

Burning spell remains is usually kept in Hoodoo for the remnants of a trick you have definitely finished with. Items disposed of in fire by a root worker tend to be those that an enemy has laid on them or on a client who found the trick and wants to dispose of it to end the spell, to break the jinx. Even better if the item explodes or sends out sparks when it is burnt, that is a good sign that the jinx has been broken.

Fire is still used to burn petitions though. If you are using a small fast-burning candle you can catch light to your paper slip petition just as the candle goes out and then drop it into a fire-proof container to burn out. The ashes from the burnt paper can then be mixed together with sachet powder to add to the power of the spell.

Within Hoodoo, fire is also seen as a way of harming someone, either by burning their name or their photograph. It is a symbol of torturing the victim.

Water

Running water literally carries away your spell; it is also a good medium for cleansing and purifying. Throwing the items from a spell into running water is a good way of enabling it to work, of setting the magic in motion. Running water is also useful for chase away spells, tricks that are used to make someone move location or leave you alone.

Running water is also useful as negative spirits can't cross it.

Tides in the ocean can be used for spells that need a long time to work. The cycles of the tide keep the spell working, the ebb and flow keeping the energy of the trick going around and around.

If you are using foot track magic and have gotten hold of some dirt from a person's footprints you can use this to draw them to you by throwing the dirt into the tide as it comes in or send them away from you as the tide goes out.

If you want to dispose of the remains of a trick in running water please remember to use only safe and biodegradable materials – don't poison our rivers or seas!

Whenever you do dispose of a trick in the water, throw it over your left shoulder and walk away, don't look back.

Earth

Burying a trick is a good way to end a spell, to stop the magic working. If the items you are burying are left-over trick remnants, they can be wrapped in newspaper and buried. Make sure any trick remnants you bury in your own garden have been positive ones; never bury negative or harmful tricks in your own yard.

Chapter 17

Locations for Laying Down Tricks

The importance of crossroads in Hoodoo has been mentioned earlier in the Crossroads Magic chapter. Here are other locations frequently used for laying down tricks:

Trees

The exposed roots or hollow of a tree make an excellent place for laying down tricks. You can even hang them from the branches if you wish.

Spells hung from the branches of a tree are generally positive wish tricks; you can make them pretty and decorative as they will be seen. However, there are also many Hoodoo tricks that involve nailing items to a tree with the intent of harm or death.

Hiding your trick in the roots of a tree or inside a hollow is usually for harmful spell working. Hiding the trick means it won't be found and will continue to do its work unhindered.

Graveyards

If you decide that you seriously want to cause some harm to a person your trick would be best suited for burying in a graveyard. This is for serious curses, ones that want them basically... dead. Items can also be buried in the graveyard to bring blessings to the home and fertility.

Clothing and Objects

Tricks can be laid onto the clothing of the intended person. Sachet powders can be sprinkled on a person's clothing or bed linen, anointing oils can be put on furniture or objects that they regularly touch and goofer dust or crossed pins can be placed in items of their clothing too.

Bedding is an excellent place to lay a trick. You can add goofer dust around the bed or put healing mojo bags under the mattress, add love powder sachets inside the pillow... you get the idea.

Food and Drink

Laying a trick using food or drink is quite simple. Bodily fluids can be easily added to drinks, magical herbs can be put into foods. Although adding bodily fluids to food and drink is a traditional part of Hoodoo magic, I personally would not advocate this because of the infection risk. When you lay down the trick using food or drink, state the name of the person intended, and make sure that only that person eats it.

Insects and spiders have often been used in food, ground up and made into a powder and added to the food for your intended victim, carrying harmful intent.

Doorsteps

Laying a trick at the doorstep of an intended person is usually one with evil intentions. These tricks are meant to cause an unhappy household. A bottle or box spell is often buried under the victim's doorstep or porch, so that when they enter the house they have to step over the trick, but without knowing it.

To break the jinx the spell must be dug up and broken, smashed or disposed of in fire or running water.

Earth

Burying your trick in your own garden works especially well if the spell is for your own home protection or blessing. Money draw tricks can be buried in your garden too. If you fancy raiding the laundry basket, take a pair of your partner's underwear, tie the garment in a knot and bury it in your garden, thus ensuring fidelity.

Chapter 18

What if the Magic Isn't Working?

What if your Hoodoo magic does not seem to work? There may be several reasons (as with most magical workings, not just Hoodoo).

You need to empower your words and any items that you use, your words need to have real meaning and any items used need to be charged with your intent and energy.

With any desire or wish, your outcome needs to be clearly stated or visualised. Don't faff about, don't be wishy washy – state and visualise clearly what you want to happen.

If you are sending jinxes or crossing a person and it doesn't work, it may be that they are stronger with magic than you or that they are incredibly well protected. You may need to step it up a notch.

Make sure you get your words right. Don't use double negatives, don't use conflicting statements, be very, very clear.

Be honest with what you want, be firm and be in control.

Don't keep thinking about your spell after you have laid the trick; finish it, tidy up and forget about it.

Be positive about the outcome from the start, don't think that it won't work, or it won't!

If it fails it might also be that you have been crossed yourself. Do an uncrossing, cleanse yourself and your home and start over again.

Give a trick time to work. Sometimes it may need a bit of a boost or redoing to really work or to work faster.

Chapter 19

Famous People in Hoodoo

Marie Laveau

Although generally associated with the religion of Voodoo, I want to put a bit here about Marie Laveau (often referred to as the Voodoo Queen of New Orleans). You probably can't visit New Orleans without seeing her name in the town. You will also find commercially made oils and waters bearing her name and a lot of her practice seems to have been in Hoodoo magic. I do wonder if the 'Voodoo Queen' hype was used as a marketing ploy!

There is sometimes a bit of confusion over whether she was one or two people, but there were two women, the Marie Laveau who was born around 1794 and died in 1881, and her daughter, also with the same name, who was born in 1827 and died in 1897.

The first Marie Laveau was born in Santa Domingo around 1794. She was of mixed blood, that of white, black and Indian, and was said to be beautiful. She was the daughter of a Creole planter Charles Laveau and his mistress Marguerite Darcantel. While she was young, she moved to New Orleans and was raised as a Catholic. She married in 1819 to a carpenter, Jacques Paris. They lived in a house given to them by Charles Laveau in Rampart Street. Not long after they were married her husband disappeared. No one seems sure where he went, but he wasn't seen again in New Orleans. After his departure Marie become a hairdresser to the high end society of New Orleans, and got to hear all of the latest gossip about who was seeing who and all the affairs!

In 1826 Marie become a mistress to Captain Louis Christophe Duminy de Glapion. Although they never married they lived together in Marie's house in Lampart Street and had an astounding 15 children! The eldest was named after her mother. Captain Duminy de Glapion died in 1855 and was buried in the Laveau family tomb.

Marie Laveau trained with the 'Voodoo' Doctor Jean Montaigne, often called Doctor John or John Bayou. He was a well known Voodoo practitioner although again I wonder if it was more towards Hoodoo, as many male Hoodoo practitioners call themselves 'Doctor'. She learnt how to work with herbs and remedies and how to make charms, potions and mojo bags. This all added extra services to her hairdressing as she was able to offer a sideline to her affluent customers, providing readings, predictions, charms or hexes as required. Eventually she gave up the hairdressing business and concentrated on her magical skills.

Marie gathered around her a network of spies made up of slaves and servants who worked in local houses belonging to the wealthy section of society. They all reported back to her with the current gossip and scandal, so she always knew what was going on. With all of this knowledge she became a powerful source of information who the rich people came to for advice, which she happily dispensed, for a sum of money of course.

Congo Square was the 'in' place for rituals, worship and ceremonies involving dancing and drumming. That spread to Lake Pontchartrain, which Marie took over the control of initially, eventually taking over Congo Square too. This was actually quite a brave thing to do because it was illegal for black people to congregate there.

She made a fortune charging people for her services and ceremonies, but it seems she also donated a lot to the poor and needy too. In 1853 New Orleans was hit by an epidemic of yellow fever. Marie Laveau was instrumental in fighting it, ministering to those who were ill. She would also visit prisoners and sit and pray with them, or minister to them if they were sick.

She acquired a house in St Anne Street, which she filled with many Voodou and spiritual items. This house later became the residence for her eldest daughter Marie Laveau.

One of the most well known stories was that of a local businessman J B Langrast who hated what Marie Laveau did and all she stood for. He started blaming her and her followers for every murder or theft that occurred. Marie soon got fed up with this and Mr Langrast started to find mojo bags with unpleasant contents on his doorstep. He started to appear to lose his mind and eventually left New Orleans worried that his life was in danger...

In 1875 Marie Laveau announced she was retiring. A few years later she moved in to the St Anne Street house so that her eldest daughter could care for her. She passed away on 15th June 1881.

There was so much hype created about her and there are so many myths and legends, it is difficult to pick the truth out from the stories, but she must have been an incredible woman.

Her daughter Marie Laveau gradually took over her mother's business – fuelling the myth that Marie Laveau the elder had perpetual youth, when in fact it was her daughter appearing at the ceremonies and rituals pretending to be her.

Marie Laveau the younger also started out as a hairdresser like her mother. She was also tall and beautiful. She went on to run a bar and a brothel on Bourbon Street, which was good experience for eventually taking over from her mother.

She continued to organise rituals and ceremonies as her mother had done, looking after the needs of the high society. But she too tended to the poor when they were sick and needy.

However, I don't believe she ever gained the same status that her mother did.

It is said that she drowned in 1897 during a storm, other stories say she died of a heart attack.

Doctor Jean Montaigne/Doctor John/John Bayou

Doctor John's story was that he was enslaved by the Spanish and taken to Cuba, where after working hard his master set him free.

He then travelled the world as a sailor, but on stopping at New Orleans he decided to stay. His magical skills soon grew in fame and he quickly became a wealthy man. He bought himself a large house on Bayou road and acquired several slaves whom he then married and fathered it is said, up to 50 children.

King Solomon

King Solomon is a key figure in Hoodoo. You will often find oil and incense blends with his name on them. The Biblical figure was known for his great wisdom and magical skills, he also owned a huge array of magical and protective items and was said to have been able to command demons and spirits. He was also a powerful leader and judge. He had 700 wives and 300 concubines (he must have been a busy man!) and he is also said to have had an affair with the Queen of Sheba. He is said to have been a King of Israel, one of the 48 prophets and son of David. He is credited with being the man who oversaw the building of the first temple in Jerusalem.

There are medieval grimoires in existence which state him to be the author. In these books he is portrayed as an astronomer, a poet and a magician (although I think in reality a lot of these books were written much later but were inspired by his works). These books contain seals, sigils, pentacles and talismans for use to invoke the power of demons, spirits, angels and the planets.

Chapter 20

Hoodoo Deities and Spirits

As I mentioned before, Hoodoo is a magical practice and not a religion. However, because a lot of its practitioners follow religions it seems to have incorporated elements from various religions along the way, including deities, spirits and saints. These deities or spirits are worshipped or served in various religions such as Santeria, Candomblé, Arara, Yoruba and many others. In Santeria and Yoruba they are referred to as Orishas and in Vodou they are called Loa or Lwa. In Hoodoo it is the saints that are often called on, but you will find all across the internet and in occult stores candles, oils and powders referring to the Orishas and Loas, so for reference I have included some information about some of the main deities, spirits and saints. It is by no means a comprehensive list.

Within my own spiritual path I don't see any problem in working with deities or spirits from any pantheons or religions; that is my own personal belief. I have worked a lot with Celtic deities, but also with those from the Greek, Roman and Hindu pantheons and I have also worked with Orishas. I want to stress here that I mean no disrespect to any of the religions, if a spirit or deity makes itself known to me and wishes to teach me I will be guided by them. What I would advise is doing some research yourself before working with Orishas or Loas, they are very powerful and you should take measures of protection before doing do. Knowledge is power as they say. In fact with any deities, saints or spirits that you petition, it is wise to be polite, courteous and respectful – they aren't there to do your dirty work for you and they won't necessarily want to work with you! Remember that each saint, each Orisha, each Loa needs to be honoured properly and in specific ways. If you choose to do so, do your research!

In my own personal journey I have been working with Papa Legba on a regular basis over the past year or so. He is definitely a 'character' and loves to have tobacco and rum left on the altar for him. He likes to laugh but has a definite serious side to him too. I have learnt a lot from him and benefited from his knowledge and guidance.

Saints

Saint Peter

Opens the way for you to get things that you need, but also closes doors to your enemies. Saint Peter will also close doors to you if you don't keep your word. He is also called upon for justice and success.

Saint Anthony

Helps with the recovery of lost or stolen items and also helpful in finding new jobs or partners. He is also the protector of children and the poor.

Saint Jude

Saint Jude can be called upon when you are in a desperate situation, when all else has failed. He is the patron saint of lost causes. He can be requested when miracle healing is needed.

Saint Martha the Dominator

Saint Martha works well with victimised or abused women and men. She can be called upon to dominate and control people and situations. She is a good saint to call upon for break-up spells and to defeat your enemies.

Saint Michael

Saint Michael can be petitioned by anyone whose heart is in the right place. He can bring strength and support. Also, he is a good saint to call upon for protection.

Orishas

Eleggua

Eleggua was the first Orisha created by Olodumare. He is the key to religious practices. His blessing is required to start a ritual and indeed to proceed and succeed in life. He is the owner of all roads, crossroads and doorways. He allows all prayers to reach the Orishas. He likes to test humanity to see what they will do next.

Babluaye

Spirit of sickness, healing and provider for the poor, spirit of the Earth, he is also associated with the sun. Babluaye is known as Lord of Smallpox. He is a strong fit looking man but he is lame in one leg so usually walks with the aid of a staff. Despite the connection with sickness and disease Babluaye is a jolly fellow full of mercy with a good sense of humour and, when needed, he will bring peace. He is to be respected, but also feared as he not only brings cures, he can also bring illness.

Ogun

Lord of tools, birds and beasts, hunting and politics. He influences wars, battles, soldiers, blacksmiths, farming, transportation and healing. He is also the spirit of metal. Ogun is strong and powerful, very masculine, he is a warrior that isn't afraid of hard work or getting his hands dirty. He likes to work with his hands whether it is farming or blacksmithing. He is also a good Orisha to call upon if you have car or mechanical problems. He is another Orisha that loves his family very much. He gives strength through prophecy and magic.

Ochosi

Ochosi is a hunter. He stalks his prey and gives out blind justice to all. He also opens and clears roads.

Obatala

Bringer of peace and harmony, creator of human bodies. He is the father figure of the Orishas, chief and judge. His wife is Yemaya. He influences knowledge, leadership, fatherhood, justice, protects the handicapped and aids in legal matters. He is a symbol of peace and purity. He rules the mind and intellect and balance.

Santeria beliefs say that Obatala made all human beings. Unfortunately, while he was in the process he started drinking some wine, and then some more, and then a bit too much. While he was drunk he made some of the humans with disabilities, when he sobered up he was very sorry and has never drunk a drop of alcohol since and swore to protect handicapped people.

Oya

Warrior, goddess of wind, lightning, fertility and fire and guardian of the Underworld. She influences the weather, creates tornadoes and hurricanes, death, cemeteries, business, changes and witchcraft. Her full name Oya-Yansan means 'mother of nine'. She often wears disguises and masks. She is strong willed, efficient and excellent in emergencies.

Oshun

Oshun is the goddess of water, beauty, wealth, diplomacy, intimacy, maternity and love. She influences all fresh water, love, pregnancy, romance, witchcraft and healing. Oshun is beautiful, full of character, generosity and kindness. She is a happy and joyful Orisha, full of laughter and love. She is life itself, all the good things. She is the unseen mother present at every gathering. She understands cosmic forces, making her omnipresent and omnipotent. Oshun works witchcraft and especially love, fertility and wishing spells.

But do be warned that Oshun has a dark side too (don't we all?), because she loves so much she often has her heart broken, she can be vain and jealous along with being insecure and petty. She also has a very short attention span.

Yemaya

Spirit of motherhood, goddess of the ocean and the moon, she watches over family issues, pregnancy, children and healing. Yemaya gives life to the ocean, the shore line and the coasts. Legend says that Yemaya gave birth to the 14 Yoruban goddesses and gods. When her waters broke it caused a great flood, creating the oceans. The first human man and woman were borne from her womb. Yemaya was the Orisha that protected all the slaves as they were transported across the ocean. She is very kind and generous and does not get upset easily, although if you do push her too far you will see the full force of her might. Family is extremely important to Yemaya especially looking after and caring for children.

Shango

God of Thunder, fire and lightning and sensuality. He influences protection, magic, life, justice and virility.

Shango is the party animal bad boy of the Orishas. He is a real man, hot, fiery and sexy. He likes a good fight and a good drink. He is also a very talented sorcerer. He is most definitely not a deity to connect with the dead or the after life – he is all about life and living for the moment. He has the power to help you win wars, defeat your enemies and gain power over others. He ensures victory of all kinds. Treat him as you would a king. He can bring you great power and self control.

Orunmila

Orunmila is the Orisha of divination; he also deals with destinies, knowledge, wisdom and fate. He is often shown as a wise old black man with grey hair and carries a diviner's tray.

Eshu

Eshu understands evil. It is said that when evil first came into the world, the Orishas didn't know what to do, so Eshu sacrificed half of himself so that he became half evil – in doing so he understands how man thinks of evil and therefore Eshu understands how to deal with it. He influences communication, crossroads, doorways, sex and protection.

Eshu echoes the dark side of our soul, he is present when black magic or drugs are involved. He is the weakness in our wills.

Ibeji

The Ibeji are twins but are usually considered as one Orisha. They are the children of Oshun and Chango. They were the first twins to ever be born and as such their mother was shunned, so she threw out the Ibeji. Oya took in the twins and raised them. They were given the names Taiwo (a boy) and Kehinde (a girl).

Aggayu

Aggayu is related to Shango. Some say he is his father, some say he is his younger brother. Aggayu is the Orisha of volcanoes. He is also the ferry man who takes people across the river. He is also referred to as the Orisha of the desert.

Loas (Lwas)

Papa Legba

Papa Legba is the keeper of the crossroads, messenger, protector, fortune (and misfortune), the personification of death and the spirit of chaos and trickery.

He is a gatekeeper and guards the entrance to the spirit world. He has the power to remove obstacles and he provides opportunities. All ceremonies begin and end with Papa Legba, and there can be no communication with any of the other Loas without consulting him first. When a priest or priestess wishes to contact spirit they must first make a prayer to Papa Legba to open the gates to the otherworld so that the spirit may come across. All ceremonies begin with Papa Legba. His gift for linguistics enables him to translate the requests of humans into the languages of the spirits and Loas.

Papa Legba is also considered a sun spirit as he can give life. This is part of his role as the gatekeeper to the otherworld. He is a creator, he makes life and he deals with matters of order and your destiny. Offerings are made to him at crossroads as he is keeper of those too. He is also known as a storyteller.

Erzulie Dantor

Erzulie Dantor is a mother. She watches and cares for children, but she is also a disciplinarian and does not tolerate badly behaved children. She will defend women, families and children to the very end. She can also be petitioned for love, art, jealousy and sex magic.

Baron Samedi

Spirit of the dead, sex, resurrection and endings. Although he is a Loa of death he is also a big party animal and he has a good if sometimes naughty sense of humour. He will also be extremely honest, if you want a no-holds-barred truth answer he is the one to give it. He advises us to respect the dead and asks that we make sure that we honour our inner happiness too. He can help with endings, not just as in death but endings of relationships and situations.

Papa Gede

Said to be the first man who ever died, Papa Gede waits at the crossroads to take souls into the afterlife. He never takes a life before its time and always protects children. He knows everything that goes on in all worlds.

Maman Brigitte

Loa of the dead (wife to Baron Samedi), protector of gravestones, she is queen of the cemetery and a fair and just judge. She has a fiery personality and is a very passionate woman who likes a drink and curses quite a lot!

Ayizan

She is a rot Loa and covers rites of initiation and is regarded as the first priestess. She covers knowledge, mysteries and the natural world.

Agwe

Agwe rules over the sea and all that is contained within it and all and everyone who sails on it.

The Seven Powers of Africa

The Seven Powers of Africa refer to the seven most well known and celebrated Orishas of the Yoruban pantheon. Deities in the religion of Santeria are referred to as Las Sietes Potencias, in Candomblé and Umbanda they are called Orixa, in Voudoun they are called Loas (Lwas) and in Palo they are referred to as Nkisi.

The seven consist of Eleggua, Obatala, Yemaya, Oya, Oshun, Chango, Ogun, Orula and Babluaye.

Chapter 21

Religions

Now I know I have made it quite clear that Hoodoo is not a religion, but a magical practice used by many religions. It does incorporate elements of Christianity, but it is also a part of Yoruba, Santeria, Vodoun and Candomblé, so I wanted to share a little bit of information with you about those just for reference.

Candomblé

Candomblé is an African/Brazilian religion. The word Candomblé means 'dance in honour of the gods' and indeed dance and music play a major role. Candomblé has many different elements drawn from Yoruba, Fon, Bantu and Christianity. The main deity within Candomblé is God or Oludumare and the deities are referred to as Orixas who all serve Oludumare.

Candomblé goes back to the days of the slave trade when Africans were shipped to Brazil. They were not allowed to follow their own faith and instead were forced to convert to Christianity (familiar story here). However, they kept their original beliefs and just incorporated them or disguised them within the Catholic religion they were made to follow.

Every person has a personal Orixa who helps them to carry out their own destiny. Their Orixa aids them, advises them and protects them. Orixas are spirit gods that link humans to the spiritual world. Each Orixa is connected to a force in nature and each person's personality is a reflection of their own Orixa.

Santeria

Santeria is an Afro-Caribbean religion that evolved from the Cuban slave trade. It is also referred to as La Regla Lucumi.

Santeria means 'worship of the saints'. It is based on African traditions, but also incorporates some elements of Christianity.

Africans from Benin and Nigeria were sent to Cuba to become part of the slave trade. Their Yoruba traditions were kept in the main but added to with some of the Christian traditions.

Santeria has Orishas who are spirit manifestations of God or Olodumare. The Orishas help people throughout their daily lives; they also help people reach their destiny. The deal is that the Orishas help the people so long as the people worship the Orishas, the worship sustains the Orishas. The Roman Catholic elements can be seen in Santeria by the belief in Catholic saints and symbols.

Voudoun/Vodou/Voodoo

Haitian Vodou is a creolised religion with roots in Dahomean, Kongo, Yoruba and other areas of Africa. Slaves were brought to Saint Domingue (as Haiti was known then) and Christianised by Roman Catholic missionaries. The word Vodou means 'spirit' or 'deity'. The main deity is Bondye but he does not interfere with human affairs so they serve spirits called Loas. Each Loa has a specific personality, abilities and characteristics. Each person can connect with a specific Loa to help them through particular areas of their life, if they like you!

Yoruba

Yoruba covers Southwestern Nigeria and parts of Benin and Togo. The faith of Yoruba is also known as Aborisha or Orisha-Ifa. The great divinity is Obatala and was chosen by Olodumare to create the Earth and all its people.

The beliefs are that each person is possessed by an Ayanmo (a destiny) and that eventually each person will become one with Olodumare, the divine creator and source of all. The goal for each person is to live their life doing good and to grow spiritually. The spirits are called Orishas or Oris. The word Ori means 'head' and literally translates as your spiritual intuition and destiny. By working with your Orishas you can spiritually and physically bring about healing and find balance and inner peace in your life.

Glossary of Terms/Words Used in Hoodoo

Anointing oil: oil blend used to enhance the power of candles and other objects.

Ashe: the magical life force energy in all things.

Banishing: a trick to remove negative energy or people.

Botanica: an occult store carrying spiritual supplies.

Black magic: dark spells involving causing harm and hurt to others.

Charging: sending energy into an item to strengthen your intent.

Conjure: to draw magic, spirits or energy.

Crossroads: a magical 'in between' place where four roads intersect.

Curse: negative energy sent to someone.

Doll baby: another name for a poppet.

Dressing: to add magical energy to candles using oils.

Essential oil: a plant essence extracted from flowers, leaves, stems, berries or roots.

Feeding powder: a blend of substances ground together and used to sustain the life force energy of an object.

Fixing tricks: working spells.

Flannel: material bag used to make a mojo bag.

Foot track magic: an element of Hoodoo that involves tracks or footprints of someone.

Gris gris: another word for a mojo bag.

Laying of tricks: Hoodoo term for working spells.

Mojo: bag filled with ingredients used as an amulet.

Nation sack: a female owned mojo bag.

Poppet: a stuffed doll used to represent a person.

Root work: another name for the practice of Hoodoo.

Trick: Hoodoo name for a spell.

Veve: drawing used to invoke the spirit of a deity.

Vodoun: religious path.

Sources for Further Research

Note: I am not responsible for the content of any of the following websites!

www.oldstyleconjure.com
www.luckymojo.com
www.stephanierosebird.com
www.thedemoniacal.blogspot.co.uk

If you get the chance to have a look at any of the Hyatt's Hoodoo Conjuration Witchcraft Rootwork books they are fascinating. However, they are very expensive.

Moon Books invites you to begin or deepen your encounter with Paganism, in all its rich, creative, flourishing forms.